Album of
Sharks

ALBUM OF SHARKS

AMONG THE MANY misconceptions about sharks is the belief that they are vicious hunters of people. Certainly most sharks are extremely dangerous, and many have been known to attack and kill human beings. But no shark deliberately seeks out human flesh. Instead, their tastes are more eclectic. Among the indigestibles found within tiger sharks, for example, are a roll of tar paper, a keg of nails, three overcoats, and a chicken coop complete with a few bones and feathers! Yet the largest of all sharks feeds mainly on plankton, and another sits camouflaged on the sea bottom, quietly *waiting* for its food to approach.

Introducing us to a wide variety of the 250 species of sharks, the same author-artist team that collaborated on the popular ALBUM OF DINOSAURS and ALBUM OF PREHISTORIC ANIMALS joins forces on this book. Together, Tom McGowen and Rod Ruth take us well beyond the shark stereotype. While no book on the subject would be complete without such fierce killers as the great white shark and the hammerhead, so it would be lacking without sharks like the sluggish wobbegong and the huge though practically harmless whale shark. Large and small, treacherous and gentle—the variety of sharks presented here is great.

But ALBUM OF SHARKS does more than survey the characteristics and habits of many of these fish. A great deal of general information is presented, as are many anecdotes about these much-maligned creatures. We learn about the characteristic feeding frenzy, as well as how sharks differ from other fish. On a lighter note we discover how one shark provided key evidence in a murder mystery, and how another, according to legend, teamed up with swordfish to kill whales. Finally we are introduced to an array of strange sharks that range from a prehistoric "leftover" to one that glows in the dark.

Sharks in all their shapes and sizes are fascinating creatures, and ALBUM OF SHARKS, a meticulously researched, colorfully illustrated volume, does them justice.

Album of Sharks

By TOM McGOWEN

Illustrated by ROD RUTH

CHECKERBOARD PRESS

New York

Text and illustrations reviewed and
authenticated by William P. Braker,
Director, John G. Shedd Aquarium,
Chicago, Illinois

To Jamie

Library of Congress Cataloging-in-Publication Data
McGowen, Tom.
  Album of sharks.
  Reprint. Originally published: © 1977.
  Includes index.
  Summary: A general introduction to sharks with
specific descriptions of twelve different kinds.
  1. Sharks—Juvenile literature. [1. Sharks]
I. Ruth, Rod. ill. II. Title.
QL638.9.M34 1987   597'.31   87-11642
ISBN 0-02-688513-1

CHECKERBOARD PRESS and colophon are trademarks of Macmillan, Inc.

Contents

Sharks!

A HUGE, sleek, torpedo-shaped body gliding menacingly through the blue water above a coral reef. Giant jaws bristling with razor-sharp teeth. A fierce hunger that may suddenly explode into a savage, slashing attack! That's the picture that enters the minds of most people when they first hear the word *shark*. They think of a shark as being a very big, fast, meat-eating fish that often attacks people. But just how true *is* that picture?

To begin with, there isn't just one kind of creature called shark. There are about 250 different kinds, or species of them, living in all the oceans of the world. And

while a few kinds of sharks do fit the picture of the big, sharp-toothed, fast-moving hunter, a great many do not. For not all sharks *are* big—there are a number of kinds of them that are little more than a foot long, and one kind is only a little more than 5 inches long. Not all sharks are fast moving —there are some that usually move so slowly they seem to be half-asleep, and some that spend most of their time simply lying motionless on the sea bottom. And, not all sharks are razor toothed. Some have narrow, cone-shaped, pointed teeth, and there's one kind with back teeth that are much like a single, jagged lump of concrete.

So, sharks are actually a very large group of many different kinds of creatures, with many different ways of life. They are fish, but they are all different from other fish in several ways—and these differences are what *make* them sharks.

For one thing, while sharks have gills, as do most other fish, a shark's gills aren't covered like those of other fish. Sharks can be recognized by their gill slits, which are long, straight openings on each side of their bodies, just behind their heads. Most kinds of sharks have five of these slits, but some have six, and some have seven.

Creatures with gills breathe by taking

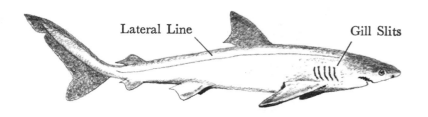

Lateral Line   Gill Slits

oxygen out of the water that passes over their gills. Most fish are able to pump water over their gills, but many kinds of sharks cannot do this. In order to breathe, then, they must *constantly* swim, taking water into their mouths, where it passes over their gills and then goes out through the gill slits. If these sharks should stop swimming, they would sink to the sea bottom and die of suffocation. They must, literally, swim for their lives.

Other differences between sharks and other fish may be seen in their skeletons and their scales. Fish, like mammals, reptiles, amphibians, and birds, have skeletons that are formed of bone. But a shark's skeleton is made of cartilage, or what most people call gristle. As for a shark's scales, they are actually like nothing less than millions of tiny teeth sticking up out of the skin. If you were to rub your hand over any kind of shark's skin, it would feel as if you were rubbing sandpaper, whereas the skin of most fish feels smooth and slimy. In years past, carpenters and other woodworkers used sharkskin as sandpaper.

Sharks differ from other fish in still another way. Most fish lay enormous amounts of soft, jellylike eggs, but most kinds of sharks give birth to fully formed babies. Those that don't, lay eggs with hard coverings. Thus, it is all these things—method of birth, gill slits, a cartilaginous skeleton, scales like teeth, and differences in the body both inside and out—that make a shark a shark. Size, speed, and sharp teeth are not the only shark traits.

While a great many kinds of fish feed only on plant life, all sharks are strictly meat eaters. However, different kinds of sharks eat different kinds of "meat." Some eat mainly shellfish, such as crabs and clams. Many small and medium-sized sharks feed on small fish, such as herring and mackerel. One of the very biggest sharks eats nothing but the very *smallest* creatures in the sea— the tiny plants and animals that make up the huge, drifting masses of life called plankton. And some kinds of large sharks will eat *any* kind of animal food they can get—small fish; large fish such as rays, swordfish, and other sharks; turtles; seabirds; seals; porpoises; and any dead creature they may find floating in the water.

Sharks have plenty of "equipment" to help them find their food. Like most kinds of fish they have what is known as a lateral line system, which is a group of tubes just under the skin, filled with thick, gluey fluid. One of these tubes runs along each side of the shark's body, and several others are located in the head. These tubes enable the shark to feel the vibrations caused by an injured, floundering fish or other creature that is as much as 100 feet away. The shark's sense of smell can pick up the odor of blood in the water from about one quarter of a mile away, and a shark can hear even faint sounds of movement that are as much as a thousand yards distant. Thus, a wounded, struggling fish or other creature sends out "signals" that a distant shark can quickly detect, and the scent of blood and the sound and "feel" of a creature struggling in the water can draw a shark like a magnet. As the shark approaches possible prey, its keen eyesight can locate and separate a moving object from the background at a distance of 50 feet.

Are sharks *always* seeking food? As a matter of fact, they are, although they are not always hungry and can go for a very long time—weeks, and even months—without eating. However, a shark, like any other flesh-eating animal, must always be ready to take food where it can get it, so a shark is, literally, always hunting.

Sharks have one rather strange habit that has been observed by many people. It is known as the feeding frenzy. Often, when a number of sharks gather to feast on easy prey they have located, such as a dead whale or porpoise, they will grow more and more excited as they dart in and out, seizing mouthfuls of food. Quickly this excitement becomes a crazed frenzy, with the water turning into a seething mass of sharks, foam, and blood. When sharks are in this crazed state, they will bite at anything near them—wooden boxes, tin cans, and sometimes even one another. When the prey has been devoured, the sharks begin to swim more slowly and finally calm down. Exactly what causes the feeding frenzy is not known.

Do these creatures prey on human beings? Well, humans *have* been attacked by some kinds of sharks, and humans *have* been eaten by some large sharks, so these sharks are considered to be dangerous. However, there have been many sailors and other people, who have for some reason found themselves in water filled with sharks —often for several hours—and who have not been touched. A great many divers and underwater explorers have had encounters with sharks, and they have often felt that the sharks were more afraid of *them* than they were of the sharks! The truth is simply that a big shark is a dangerous, unpredictable, wild animal searching for food. If it comes upon a hurt or helpless person—or a person that it senses is easy prey—it may well attack, just as it might attack a helpless fish or other creature. But *no* shark deliberately swims around *looking* for humans to eat!

The twenty or so kinds of sharks you will read about in this book run the gamut from "typical" sharks, such as the blue shark, to relatively little-known creatures like the lantern shark and the frilled shark. A great many of the more common kinds of sharks, such as the lemon shark and the whitetip, are not mentioned because their way of life is similar to that of sharks like the blue or mako, both of which are fully covered.

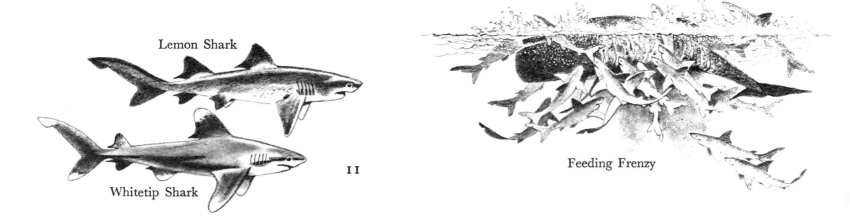

Lemon Shark

Whitetip Shark

11

Feeding Frenzy

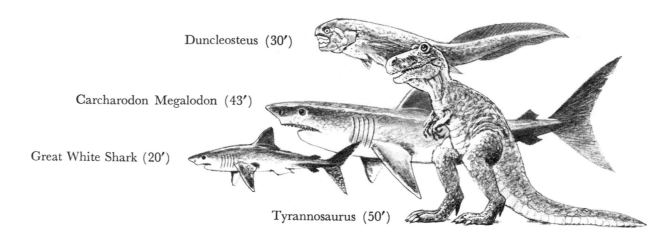

Duncleosteus (30')

Carcharodon Megalodon (43')

Great White Shark (20')

Tyrannosaurus (50')

The Great White Shark

IN EVERY age since life appeared on earth, there has always been at least one creature that was "king" of all the flesh-eating animals of its time—one creature that exceeded all others in size and ferocity. The "king," 350 million years ago, was a 30-foot-long armored fish with jagged jaws like the beak of a snapping turtle. Seventy million years ago, it was the 50-foot-long dinosaur, *Tyrannosaurus*. And 20 million years ago, it was a 43-foot-long shark.

This huge creature has been named *Carcharodon megalodon* (kar-KAR-uh-dahn MEHG-uh-luh-dahn), which means, "rough tooth, giant tooth." It was a swift, sleek, mountain of muscle that must have been one of the most deadly killers ever to inhabit the earth. Its teeth were arrow-shaped slicing tools, 4 inches long, and when the jaws that contained those teeth were opened to their widest measure, as many as *six* people could have *stood* within them!

This enormous, terrifying creature has, fortunately, long been extinct. But its descendant, a creature very much like it in every way, only smaller, roams the seas today. It, too, is called *Carcharodon*, but it is more commonly known as the great white shark—or, man-eater.

Although the great white shark is much smaller than its giant ancestor, it is one of the largest flesh-eating animals in the world now. However, it is, perhaps, not quite as large as many people have thought. Careful measurements by scientists seem to show that most white sharks probably reach an average size of about 17 feet, while some may be a little more than 20 feet in length. In all other respects, the great white shark is probably much like its ancestor. Its big mouth is abristle with triangle-shaped teeth that have saw-toothed edges that can slice through flesh like a steak knife cuts through a chunk of beef. In the largest white sharks, the teeth may be as much as 3 inches long.

White sharks are tough, powerful animals with an incredible ability to survive. In 1964, off the coast of New York, Captain Frank Mundus, a professional shark fisherman, caught one of the largest white sharks taken in this century—and it took him five hours, five harpoons, and fifteen bullets to do it! The shark was more than 17 feet long, and when Mundus spotted it from the deck of his boat, *Cricket,* he knew it could not be caught with a hook and line. So he harpooned it. The shark raced away, attached to the boat by the hundreds of feet

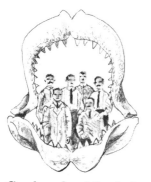

Carcharodon Megalodon Jaws

Carcharodon Tooth

12

GREAT WHITE SHARK

of sturdy line on the harpoon. Mundus, in the boat, followed slowly, letting the shark tire itself out. After an hour, Captain Mundus began to pull the shark in, and when it was close enough, hurled another harpoon into it. Again, the shark went racing away, now with two harpoons in its body, and again Mundus and the *Cricket* followed. It took four more hours and three more harpoons before the shark stopped "running" and *Cricket* could tow it to shore.

Then, it took a bulldozer to haul the huge creature up onto the beach, and while this was being done, a crowd of more than a hundred excited people gathered. Suddenly, the shark "came to life" again, beginning to twitch and move its tail. Fearful that someone might be hurt by a sudden blow of the massive tail, Captain Mundus got his rifle and shot the creature in the head, using 15 bullets before he was certain that the big shark was finally and positively dead!

Despite its common name, the great white shark is not actually white. Young sharks of this species have brownish backs that become grayish or bluish as the sharks grow older. This color gradually shades to a dingy white on the shark's sides and underbelly. The shark actually gets its name from the color of its belly, although many other kinds of sharks have whiter bellies than it does.

Apparently rather rare, white sharks are "lone wolves," keeping to themselves rather than swimming in schools, or groups, as some other kinds of sharks do. They roam the open sea in all parts of the world, preferring the warm, southern seas, but moving northward when summertime comes to the northern part of the earth. They eat all kinds of fish, large and small; sea turtles; porpoises; seals; other smaller sharks; and most any dead animal they find, including whales. They sometimes follow ships in order to eat the garbage that is thrown overboard. Like several other kinds of sharks, they are apparently willing to try almost anything, and the stomach of one of them was found to contain a tin can, a number of sheep bones, the front part of a bulldog, the back part of a pig, and some chunks of horseflesh.

White sharks are also supposed to be eaters of humans, which is why they are called "man-eaters" in most parts of the world, as well as "death sharks" in Australia. Stories of their horrifying attacks on humans have been told for hundreds of years. Many scientists of several hundred years ago were sure that the creature that was supposed to have swallowed Jonah, in the Bible story of Jonah and the whale, was actually a great white shark. It was claimed by several writers of the fifteenth and sixteenth centuries that white sharks had been caught which, when cut open, were found to have the bodies of men in full armor inside them! In modern times, the stories of these creatures are no less frightening. It is claimed that white sharks will often attack boats, smashing them to splinters in order to get at the people aboard them. There are stories of these sharks leaping onto boats to seize sailors, and lurking off the coasts near beaches where people go swimming, in hopes of catching a plump, tasty human!

14

How true are all these tales? *Can* a white shark swallow someone whole? *Do* they deliberately attack boats? *Are* these giant fish the vicious man-eaters they are reputed to be?

A 20-foot-long white shark *can* swallow a human whole. A few white sharks *have* been found with the body of a human being in their stomachs. However, in every case, doctors found that the people had drowned long before the sharks actually swallowed them. In other words, the sharks had simply happened to come across a floating object and had gulped it down. There is no record of a white shark ever swallowing anyone alive.

White sharks *have* attacked boats. But most scientists feel that the sharks probably thought that the boats were big fish. No shark is smart enough to understand that there might be people aboard a boat. In 1953, near Nova Scotia, a large white shark attacked and smashed a small fishing boat, but then completely ignored the boat's two crewmen who were in the water for several hours. Obviously, the shark hadn't attacked the boat to get the men.

White sharks *have* attacked swimmers. However, it actually seems as if these sharks make fewer attacks on humans than do some other species of sharks, such as bull sharks. In parts of South Africa and Australia, where shark attacks are considered to be a problem and where they are studied, there often were no known attacks by white sharks for years on end.

The great white shark *is* dangerous. But it is dangerous mainly because it is a very large, meat-eating animal that will eat anything. Therefore, its reputation as a bloodthirsty hunter of human beings may be largely undeserved!

The Hammerhead Shark

A HOT, midmorning sun sparkled on the clear, green waters of the Gulf of Mexico. A sloop lay anchored near a small island, and the two men who made up the sloop's entire crew were lowering a dinghy—a small boat—into the water. As they finished this task, one of the men glanced out at the sparkling surface stretching away from the sloop, and his eyes widened in surprise. "Hey, look!" he urged, pointing out over his companion's shoulder.

The water close to the sloop was boiling with activity. A number of large shapes could be seen moving swiftly near the surface. Suddenly, one of the shapes shot up into the air and fell back with a resounding splash. The men recognized it as a hammerhead shark—a big one, nearly 14 feet long.

In an effort to better see what was causing this strange commotion, the two sailors scrambled to the top of the sloop's cabin and peered down into the water. They were astounded to see that the shark was being *attacked* by at least a dozen bottle-nosed porpoises that had the big fish surrounded. Every few moments, one of the porpoises would dart at the hammerhead, trying to smash into it like a battering ram!

Although porpoises, which are often called dolphins, look like big fish, they are actually mammals, like dogs, cats, horses, and humans. Swift, smart animals, they are friendly to human beings. Apparently, they are often attacked by sharks, and vicious battles between sharks and porpoises have frequently been seen. Unfortunately, the porpoises usually seem to get the worst of these encounters.

But these porpoises were obviously winning this battle against the hammerhead. Although the shark was bigger than any of them, and its savage teeth had slashed several of the porpoises' bodies, reddening the water with their blood, the men could see that the shark was weakening. Though the porpoises' small teeth were no match for the terrible teeth of the shark, their method of attack was highly effective. Each time a porpoise's head slammed into the shark's long body, it caused severe damage to the shark's gills and internal organs. The big fish was moving more and more slowly and was clearly in distress. Finally, as a porpoise came crashing into it, it gave another convulsive leap, then began to float lifelessly down into the green depths. A few porpoises followed it for a short distance, bumping it with their heads as if to make sure it was

16

HAMMERHEAD SHARK
Bottle-Nosed Porpoises

Sphyrna Tudes

Sphyrna Blochii

Sphyrna Tiburo

Sphyrna Diplana

Sphyrna Corona

really dead. Then they rejoined the others and swam away into the distance.

The men, who a number of years ago witnessed this strange drama of the sea, had no idea of what might have caused it. Perhaps the porpoises had simply banded together to rid themselves of an enemy that had been preying on them.

The hammerhead shark, the kind of shark that the porpoises killed, is a strange-looking creature. It seems almost as if it belongs on some other world, far away in space, where living creatures are put together differently from those on earth. Although a hammerhead has a typical shark body, its head is very, very different from that of any other shark, or almost any other known creature. The front part of its head, where another shark's nose would be, is stretched out into a kind of long, flat tube that sticks out at each side. At each end of the tube is an eye and a nostril! It is from this odd tube, which looks like the head of a certain kind of hammer, that the hammerhead shark gets its name.

No one knows exactly why this shark's head should be shaped in such a peculiar way. Do the widespread nostrils, far apart at each end of the tube, help a hammerhead pick up odors better than the closer-together nostrils of other sharks? Do its eyes, farther apart than the length of a man's outstretched arm, help it see better? Or does that long, flat, hammerhead shape at the front of its head act as a stabilizer, helping the shark to turn quickly as it swims at high speed after its prey? We simply don't know. But at any rate, because of the strange shape of its head, no one who sees a hammerhead shark could ever mistake it for anything else.

There are about 12 species of these extraordinary creatures. The biggest kinds, which are somewhat rare, are known as great hammerheads and average about 15 feet in length. The biggest great hammerhead ever caught was more than 18 feet long. A slightly smaller kind of hammerhead, known as the common hammerhead, reaches the respectable size of 12 feet or bigger. Two other kinds of hammerheads run from 10 to 12 feet, while the others are considerably smaller, only 4 or 5 feet in length.

Except for slight differences in their hammerhead tubes, all these creatures look much alike. In most species there is a sort of "dent in the tube's middle, but in one species it is perfectly straight, and in another it projects back at an angle on each side so that it resembles the swept-back wings of a jet airplane. And in still another species, the tube is curved and looks like nothing so much as a broad garden spade, which is why this species is known as the shovelhead or shovelnosed shark. It is also known, in some places, as the bonnethead.

Like the great white shark, the tiger shark, and some of its other relatives, the hammerhead shark is an ever-hungry predator that will eat almost anything it can. The smaller kinds of hammerheads feed mainly on crabs and barnacles that they find as they prowl over the sea bottom in shallow water. They also gulp down any small fish that come their way. Larger

Sea Bass

Skate

hammerheads prey, for the most part, on good-sized fish such as sea bass, skates, and anything else they can overpower—including *other* hammerheads, for which they seem to have a good appetite! A 14-foot-long female common hammerhead was once seen to eat four smaller members of her own species, each about 5 feet long, and two of which she swallowed down whole. And when she was later captured and cut open, her stomach was also found to contain the headless bodies of two 6-foot-long hammerheads that she had gobbled down in four big chunks!

But the very favorite food of the larger hammerheads is the kind of flat-bodied fish called a ray. This seems rather surprising, for many kinds of rays are really rough customers. They have long, whiplike tails armed with sharp points, called spines, which they can drive into an enemy's body. The spines are venomous and, in humans at least, can cause agonizingly painful wounds that are as dangerous as the bites of some venomous snakes. These fearsome weapons do not seem to bother a hammerhead one little bit, however. A 12-foot hammerhead that was harpooned off South Carolina was found to have 54 pointed, venomous spines of rays it had eaten, stuck in its jaws, head, back, and even inside its mouth. It was not the least bit inconvenienced by them. Hammerheads must be tough!

And do hammerheads ever eat people? Well, back in the year 1813, a big hammerhead was caught off the coast of New York. When the shark was cut open by the sailors who had caught it, they were horrified to find parts of the body of a man in the creature's belly. From that time on, hammerhead sharks have been considered dangerous to humans. In recent years, hammerheads have definitely been known to attack swimmers in waters near the United States, Mexico, and Australia. In two of these cases, the attacks resulted in the people's deaths.

Hammerheads are active and aggressive. When they themselves are attacked by men trying to harpoon them from boats, they will often turn and charge a boat head-on, smashing into it and sometimes managing to turn it over. Perhaps these sharks with the odd-shaped heads are not quite as dangerous as a great white shark, or a tiger shark, but nevertheless, dangerous they are!

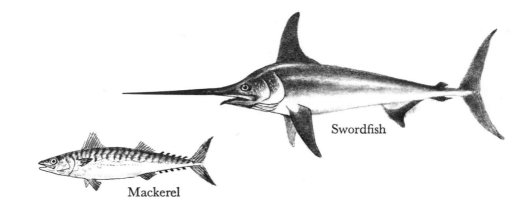

Swordfish

Mackerel

The Mako Shark

A LARGE, male broadbill swordfish was swimming lazily just beneath the sparkling surface of the ocean. Its dark, blue-gray body was more than 4 feet long, and its sword—the flat, pointed length of bone that appeared to jut straight out of its nose but was actually an extension of its upper jaw—was half as long as its body.

The swordfish was seeking prey. It was a fast-moving, aggressive creature that fed on smaller fish. It was a lord of its watery world. Because of its size, speed, and that dangerous sword that could punch right through the hull of a small boat, the swordfish had few enemies that sought it as prey.

Some distance away, a blunt, triangular fin poking up out of the water announced the presence of another creature. Its sleek body, nearly three times as long as that of the swordfish, was visible just beneath the surface of the water—a slim, torpedo shape with bright blue back and sides and a snow-white belly. This creature, too, was moving slowly, powered by the gentle, flowing, side to side motion of its tail, and guided by an occasional quick steering movement of its forward fins. But if it chose to, it could move through the sparkling water with almost incredible swiftness.

This creature was one of the swordfish's few enemies—a mako shark.

The two fish were far apart and were not aware of one another. The swordfish was moving north, along a broad, curving path; the shark was following an almost straight line, heading south.

Abruptly, the swordfish began to move faster. It had sighted motion in the water ahead. A big school of mackerel was moving near the surface—a great cloud of gleaming blue-green bodies. These fish, about a fourth the size of the swordfish, were its prey. It launched itself in an attack.

The swordfish flashed into the crowd of mackerel like a pirate swinging a cutlass, lashing about its broad head and punching with its sword. At the onslaught of the bigger fish, the mackerel began to move closer together, as if seeking protection from one another. But this merely made things easier for the swordfish. In just a few moments, a number of the mackerel were stunned, slashed, and pierced by the lashing, punching sword. As the rest of the school hurried on their way, those that had fallen victim to the swordfish were left behind, some drifting aimlessly in death, others writhing and flopping. A faint pink film of blood

Atlantic Mackerel

MAKO SHARK

Swordfish

spread out in the water, almost instantly becoming invisible.

In the distance, the mako shark began to move faster. Its sensitive body was suddenly picking up "signals." Through the water it could "feel" the floundering movement of helpless creatures, and through the water came the attractive, inviting scent of blood. Growing ever more excited, the shark rushed toward the source of these signals.

The swordfish, whose rush had carried it through the school of mackerel, now turned back to feed on the fish that had fallen to its attack. Moving quickly, it went from fish to fish, swallowing them down.

Intent on its feeding, it did not see or sense, until it was too late, the mako shark that suddenly rushed upon it. The mako's jaws sprang open in an enormous, incredible gape. The whole rear half of the swordfish's body disappeared into that frightful cavern! The mako's teeth clamped down for a moment, then, with a convulsive movement of its head, it swallowed the entire swordfish—sword and all!

The mako's rush carried it on past the point of the encounter, then it whipped its body around, and sped back and forth, snapping at the occasional drifting or floundering mackerel that were still left. Slowly, the shark's excitement subsided. It pointed its nose upward and swam to the surface. Moments later, its fin could be seen gliding through the top of the water as the shark headed into the vast, sparkling expanse of the ocean.

No one has ever actually seen an encounter such as this, between a mako shark and a swordfish, but there is no doubt that such encounters take place. For mako sharks have been caught that, when cut open, had the entire body of a swordfish, sword and all, in their stomachs. Unlike the razor-edged teeth of many sharks, the teeth of a mako shark are long, slender triangles with smooth edges—made for seizing prey rather than for cutting into it. A mako normally swallows its captives whole, no matter what their size.

The mako shark is well fitted to single out such a tough customer as a swordfish for its prey. Makos are the swiftest of all sharks, and they grow to a length of 12 feet. They are savage predators that belong to the same family as the great white shark, and in terms of its body shape, a mako is simply a smaller, slimmer version of its powerful relative.

However, swordfish are not always easy victims of mako sharks. One of the makos that had a whole swordfish in its belly had 12 wounds in its body, which had apparently been made by the swordfish's weapon. The swordfish had obviously put up a good fight before it was eaten. And in at least one combat between a mako and a swordfish, the swordfish was the victor, for the body of a mako was once found, washed ashore on an island in the Red Sea, with the broken, 18-inch blade of a swordfish's sword plunged into it. The sword had pierced the shark's vital organs, causing death.

The mako does not feed only on swordfish. Actually, it mostly eats mackerel, herring, and other small fish, as well as squid.

And, given the chance, it will apparently feed on humans. During World War II, makos are believed to have attacked sailors whose ships had been sunk, and pilots whose planes had gone down. These sharks have also been known to attack small boats, biting into them so savagely that some of the sharks' teeth are often left, sunk deep into the wood. And in one strange incident that took place in Florida in 1953, a mako actually seemed to try to make an attack on a man who was standing on the *shore!*

The mako had moved in rather close to shore, and the man fired a spear gun at it. The shark, with the spear sticking in its body, swam quickly out into deep water and leaped into the air, shaking the spear loose. Then the mako turned, rushed back toward shore, and leaped out of the water directly toward the man who had shot it, landing on the sand in front of him! A moment later, a wave washed over the shark and it swam away out of sight. Was this just coincidence, or was the mako actually trying to wreak vengeance on the human who had attacked it? With a shark —who knows?

In addition to the great white shark, the mako has another close relative that is known as the porbeagle. That name is a combination of *porpoise* and *beagle,* and perhaps the shark was given it because it looks a bit like a porpoise and has the hunting instincts of a beagle. Although the porbeagle looks "chubbier" than the mako, it, too, is a swift swimmer and preys on schools of mackerel, herring, pilchard, as well as on cod, hake, and other fish—though not, apparently, on swordfish. It reaches a length of 12 feet, and has a dark, bluish-gray body with a white underbelly. It is considered dangerous in most parts of the world, but has never been known to attack anyone in waters near the United States.

Porbeagle

The Blue Shark

THE SUN was setting upon the Pacific Ocean, turning the sky purple and orange, and tinting the water's rough surface. A seaman aboard a merchant ship paused to peer out over the water beyond the ship's stern. Moving just beyond the silvery wake left by the ship's passage were half a dozen dark, curved, pointed objects—the back fins of sharks that were trailing after the ship like hungry dogs hoping for scraps.

The seaman spat angrily. "Devils!" he muttered. "They been followin' us for days. Either somebody's going to die or else the ship is bound for harm!"

Whenever the fins of sharks are seen following a ship far out at sea, the chances are good they are the fins of the creatures known as great blue sharks. In the deep waters of the Atlantic and Pacific oceans, there are probably more of these sharks than any other kind. Packs of blue sharks often follow ships for days, and because of this have been called "wolves of the sea." And it is an old legend of the sea that when these creatures are sighted swimming behind a ship, it is an omen of disaster—someone aboard the ship is going to die, or else the ship is going to sink!

Actually, the real reason blue sharks fol-low ships is to feed on the garbage that is thrown overboard. But sailors of long ago believed that the sharks followed ships because they somehow knew that one of the crew would die and be buried at sea—where they could get his body—or that the ship would sink and the helpless sailors would be easy pickings in the water! So, sailors hated the blue shark, and would take every opportunity to kill one when they could!

As its name indicates, the main color of a blue shark is blue. Its back is a dark blue, its sides are bright blue, and its belly is silvery white. These sharks have slim bodies and long, pointed noses. Their jaws are filled with triangle-shaped teeth that have cutting edges like the blades of saws. Blue sharks are believed to grow to as much as 20 feet in length, but the biggest one ever caught was only about 12 feet long.

Blue sharks are roamers of the deep sea and seldom come into shallow water. Great travelers, their journeys often take them far and wide. In July of 1968, scientists tagged (marked) a blue shark off the coast of Massachusetts, and four months later, the same shark was found in the West Indies, 2,700 miles away. To get there it must have

BLUE SHARKS

Whaler

traveled more than 22 miles a day, every day. These sharks can move quite fast at times; one was once clocked by scientists at a speed of 43 miles an hour.

Blue sharks feed mostly on small fish, such as herring and mackerel, as well as on squid and garbage. But they will also feed on dead or dying whales, if given the chance, and were extremely troublesome to whaling ships. When a whaling ship killed a whale, the crew began the job of cutting it up, filling the water with blood. Swarms of blue sharks would then often converge on the ship and go into a frenzy, churning the water to foam as they tried to tear off chunks of the whale's rich, red meat. Blue sharks have been known to actually hurl themselves out of the water onto a whale's body, hanging on by their teeth until they were beaten off by sailors armed with sharp-edged tools called blubber spades. And, even if a blue shark were dying after being badly injured by a blow from a blubber spade, it would keep on trying to eat until it finally sank down into the water! Because these sharks seemed to be competing with the whaling ships to get whales, the men who sailed on whaling ships long ago named them "blue whalers."

It was probably blue sharks, feeding on garbage thrown from ships, that gave rise to the belief that a shark turns over on its back in order to take a bite of something. Actually, few sharks ever do this. Most of them always stay right side up to catch the fish they eat, simply because they can see better that way. But a blue shark will sometimes rather lazily turn over on its back, almost like an acrobat performing a stunt, to snap up a tasty, floating morsel of garbage.

A strange, old legend about blue sharks, which goes back nearly two thousand years, says that these sharks are devoted parents that take good care of their young ones, showing them the best places to hunt and the easiest kinds of fish to catch. The legend also insists that when danger threatens, the adult blue shark will open her mouth and the babies will swim into their parent's throat, or even into her stomach, taking refuge there until it is safe to come out. There is no truth at all to such a tale! Someone may have seen some newborn blue sharks swimming near their mother's head, which they often do, and thought she was protecting them, but this was certainly not the case. The shark that gives birth to babies one day may well eat them the next! Sharks are *not* good parents, as wolves, lions, and other mammals are. Many kinds of baby sharks hatch from eggs and are never even seen by their mothers, and others that come out of the mother's body, instead of from an egg, are on their own from the very first.

Blue sharks belong to the family of sharks that scientists call *Carcharhinidae* (kar-kuh-REEN-uh-day), meaning "rough file," because of the creatures' teeth. But the sharks of this family are more commonly known as requiem sharks. The word *requiem* means a funeral service, and these sharks were given this name long ago because they are nearly all dangerous, and some of them have been responsible for

26

many a funeral service for someone they've killed! Some of the most feared of all sharks (aside from the great white shark, of course) belong to the requiem shark family. The deadly tiger shark is a requiem shark, as are bull sharks, lemon sharks, and the sharks called whaler sharks. All these sharks have been known to attack people. But, although the great blue shark also has a reputation as a man-eater, there are no actual records of any blue sharks ever attacking humans. Nevertheless, these sharks must be considered dangerous, and no one who knows anything about sharks will be the least bit surprised if a blue shark ever *is* positively identified as the attacker of a human. As a matter of fact, there may be at least one eyewitness account of such an attack.

Many years ago, an Englishman who lived among the people of the Gilbert and Ellice Islands, in the south Pacific Ocean, wrote a book about his experiences on these islands. He told how the islanders, who hunted tiger sharks without the slightest fear, were very much afraid of a slim, bluish, 20-foot-long shark they called *rokea* (roh-kee-uh). On one occasion, when a number of islanders in boats were fishing, one of these sharks suddenly attacked one of the boats, smashing it apart and killing one of the fishermen. From the Englishman's description, the *rokea* may well have been a blue shark.

The meat of the blue shark does not taste very good, but for hundreds of years, blue sharks and several other kinds of sharks have been hunted for their fins by fishermen of China and other Far Eastern lands. The fins are used for making a delicacy of which you may have heard—shark fin soup. The fins are cut off the sharks' bodies and dried in the sun or over a fire. To make the soup, the dried fins are cooked in broth with mushrooms, pieces of chicken, and spices. Shark fin soup is served in many Chinese restaurants in the United States and other Western countries, but the soup is now usually made from the fin of a shark that is known as the soupfin shark.

Soupfin Shark

27

The Thresher Shark

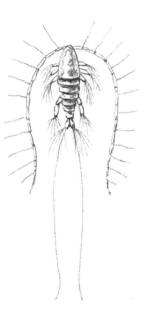

Copepod

A SCHOOL of herring was moving through the Atlantic Ocean, heading north. There were many thousands of the little foot-long fish in the school; their fine-scaled bodies, greenish-black on top and gleaming silver on the sides, gave off glints of pink and blue as they swam. It was spring—nearly time for the female herring to spawn, or lay their eggs—so the school was heading for its spawning place off the coast of northern Europe.

Days passed, and the school moved ever northward. The herring fed, as they swam, on tiny shrimplike creatures called copepods that abound in the ocean by the hundreds of billions.

In time, the coast of Europe loomed ahead like a long, gray cloud spread across the horizon. Guided by an age-old instinct, the herring headed toward the one place off this coast where, year after year, the females of this school laid their eggs, and where all the fish in the school had been hatched—near the mouth of a river. There, the river's fresh water met and mingled with the salt water of the sea.

When the school was less than a day away from its goal, it picked up a follower. The creature that now moved slowly behind it had a long, gray-black body with a blunt nose; a high, triangular back fin that cut through the surface of the water; and an enormously long tail. It was a thresher shark, or as it is sometimes called, a fox shark.

The thresher was a large one, nearly 20 feet long. But of that length, just about half was made up of the shark's incredible tail, which was shaped much like the kind of curved sword called a scimitar. The thresher swam easily, keeping pace with the school but not moving near enough to alarm any of the herring.

However, as the herring began to move into the brackish water near the mouth of the river, the thresher picked up speed. It caught up to the school, passed by it, cut in front of it, and began to swim around and around the huge mass of herring, in great circles that gradually became tighter and tighter. As it swam, it lashed the water with that enormous tail, using it like a gigantic whip!

To escape the shark's dangerously lashing tail, the herring on the outer edges of the school began to move in more closely to the others. Some of them were struck by the tail and stunned or injured. The whole

Herring

THRESHER SHARK

Atlantic Herring

school began to panic, the fish drawing closer and closer together as the shark's dark body whipped around and around them. The school became a tightly packed mass of flopping, gleaming bodies.

Then the thresher attacked! It rushed in upon the bunched-up, panic-stricken herring, snapping and gulping, its mouth writhing open and shut as it downed fish after fish. The herring did not attempt to flee from the ravaging shark, for a school of fish does not break up when it is threatened, but simply pulls closer together. Thus, the thresher was able to eat its fill.

At last, with nearly three dozen herring in its stomach, the shark was satisfied. Swimming rather slowly, it turned and headed back out toward the open sea.

The thresher shark gets its name from the way it threshes the water with its whiplike tail as it swims around and around a school of herring, mackerel, shad, or pilchard, driving them together. But it is also often called a swiveltail or swingletail, because of its supposed great skill in using its tail to actually *slap* a fish right out of the water and into its mouth! Thresher sharks have been reported to use their tails in such a way by several people. However, most scientists doubt such reports.

A number of years ago, a scientist from the Scripps Institution of Oceanography was lucky enough to get a close-up look at the way a thresher shark uses its tail to feed itself. A 6-foot-long thresher was chasing a smelt directly toward the scientist's boat, and as the man watched, the shark caught up to the fish, moved slightly ahead of it,

and then with two quick, whiplike blows of the tail, literally "knocked out" the smelt! A thresher shark was also once seen to use this tactic on an injured sea gull that was floating in the water. With a slap of its tail, the shark killed the bird, then swallowed it.

Hundreds of years ago, people believed that thresher sharks used their powerful tails to do battle against whales! Furthermore, they thought that the sharks always teamed up with a swordfish for such a battle. A book written in 1625 told how the swordfish would swim under the whale's belly while the thresher shark, swimming on the surface, would attack the whale's head, whacking away with its tail! According to the book, the whale would sink lower in the water to get away from the shark, and then the swordfish would stab it in the belly! This made the whale rise to the surface again, where the waiting thresher would start whacking away once more! The book assured its readers that such a battle might last for days, until the whale finally died from its wounds and was eaten by the two fish that had teamed up against it.

This story is completely untrue, of course. In the first place, sharks and other fish just aren't smart enough to team up in such a way. And in the second place, neither a thresher shark nor a swordfish has the kind of teeth that could even pierce a whale's hide, much less chew it! The thresher's teeth are small, smooth-edged triangles, good only for catching hold of very small fish.

It is highly doubtful that a thresher shark

would ever even waste a blow of its tail on something it couldn't eat. The thresher has never been known to strike at a human with its tail, either, and for the same reason—it couldn't eat a human.

But the people of long ago seemed to like to make up such wild tales about thresher sharks. This shark got the name of fox shark from the ancient Greeks, more than two thousand years ago, because it was supposed to be cunning, like a fox. The Greeks believed that a thresher was so clever that if it were caught by a fisherman, it would simply bite off the line and swim away. This story, too, is false. Many threshers have been caught by fishermen of today who enjoy fishing for this fast, active shark.

In addition to their other names, thresher sharks are also called long-tailed sharks, sea foxes, sea apes, rat fish, mouse fish, and peacock sharks. They are creatures of the open seas, although they often come into shallow water to prey on schools of fish. They average 13 to 16 feet in length, but may grow to as much as 20 feet, including the tail.

There seem to be about six different kinds of thresher sharks, although some scientists suspect that several of them may really all be the same. Only one kind seems vastly different from the others. It lives in deep water, rather than at the surface, and has enormous eyes, each about as big around as the rim of a drinking glass. As you may have guessed, this shark is known as the big-eyed thresher.

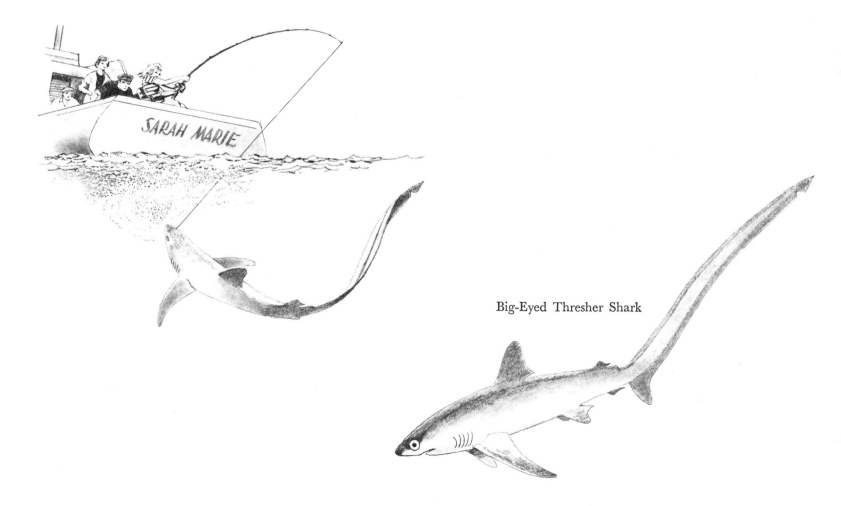

Big-Eyed Thresher Shark

The Tiger Shark

SHARKS ABOUND in the warm waters of the Hawaiian islands. They were a constant danger to the Hawaiians of long ago, who got much of their food by diving and fishing in the shark-infested waters. The Hawaiians hated and feared sharks, and many of their legends were about villainous sharks and evil shark gods and goddesses. One such legend tells how a boy named Punia (poo-nee-uh) once tricked a terrible man-eating shark.

The shark's name was Kaiuleale (ky-oo-lay-ah-lay). He was the leader of a band of ten sharks that swam in a small bay surrounded by rocky cliffs. At the bottom of one cliff was a large cave, partly filled with water, in which there was always a large number of big, tasty lobsters lying lazily on the rocks in shallow water. But none of the island people dared try to get any of these lobsters for fear of Kaiuleale and his band of sharks.

Punia and his mother, Hina (hee-nuh), lived not far from the bay. The boy had no father. His father had been a skilled fisherman, but one day out at sea his boat had been turned over by Kaiuleale's sharks, and he had been eaten. Because they had no one to fish for them, Punia and his mother had nothing to eat but sweet potatoes.

Punia often stood on the cliffs that overlooked the bay and watched Kaiuleale and the other sharks swimming slowly about with their sharp fins sticking up out of the water. It angered the boy that these sharks had killed his father and had never been punished, and it angered him that he and his mother had nothing to eat but sweet potatoes, when all those fine, big lobsters were there in the cave.

One night, Punia dreamed that his father came to him and told him what to do. As soon as he awoke, Punia said to his mother, "Today we shall have a feast! I am going to the cave of the lobsters, and I will bring back two of the biggest ones for us to eat!"

"Oh, no, Punia!" his mother cried out in dismay. "Kaiuleale and his sharks will kill you as they killed your father!"

"Don't worry, Mother," said the boy, cheerfully. "I have a plan. The spirit of my father has told me what to do."

He went down to the bay and searched until he found a large rock. Then he stood on the edge of a cliff and shouted in a loud voice, "Aha! Look at those lazy sharks! They are all asleep. I can swim into the cave and take all the lobsters I want!"

Kaiuleale chuckled evilly and whispered to the other sharks, "When you hear the splash as he dives into the water, swim toward him at once. We shall feast on the foolish boy!"

But Punia drew back his arm and with all his might threw the big stone far out to sea. When they heard it splash, all the sharks rushed out of the bay toward the place where they thought Punia had dived into the water. At once, the boy dived into the bay, swam quickly into the cave, seized two of the biggest lobsters, and was scrambling back up the rocks to the top of the cliff just as Kaiuleale and the other sharks came hurrying back.

"Punia has tricked us!" cried Kaiuleale.

"Yes!" shouted Punia. "I have two fine lobsters that I took from the cave. Kaiuleale did not catch me because the shark with the thinnest tail told me how to fool him!"

Then Kaiuleale was terribly angry. He swam around in great circles until he found the shark that he thought had the thinnest tail. He rushed at that shark, bit it in two, and gobbled up the pieces.

Up on the cliff, Punia danced for joy. "Today Kaiuleale has killed a shark instead of a boy," he cried. "And now my father is avenged!" And that day, Punia and his mother feasted on delicious lobster meat.

That old legend doesn't say what kind of a shark Kaiuleale was, but he may well have been what we now call a tiger shark. Tiger sharks are common in the waters around Hawaii, they frequently swim in groups—as Kaiuleale and his "gang" did— and they *are* man-eaters. They are every bit as dangerous as four-footed tigers. Swimmers in Australia, Florida, and other places have been attacked by tiger sharks that came into as little as 3 feet of water, no more than 10 feet from shore! A number of these attacks resulted in the deaths of the people.

Actually, though, the tiger shark did not get its name because it acts like a tiger but because the young sharks have stripes on their bodies, just as tigers do. These stripes, which are brownish on the shark's gray body, last until the shark gets to be about 6 feet long. Then, as the shark grows bigger, the stripes slowly fade and usually disappear altogether. Tiger sharks reach a size of about 18 feet.

These sharks will apparently eat almost anything! In addition to the remains of such animal food as fish, lobsters, seabirds, sea turtles, porpoises, and horseshoe crabs, the following things have been found in the stomachs of tiger sharks: a can of salmon, a leather wallet, three overcoats, a raincoat, a pair of shoes, nuts and bolts, a 2-pound coil of copper wire, cardboard boxes, cloth bags of coal, a keg of nails, a roll of tar paper, and a whole chicken coop with a few bones and feathers inside it! Several of these things were found in the stomach of the *same* shark. Apparently, as these creatures are swimming about, they will snap up anything they encounter that doesn't offer a fight.

When they can, tiger sharks also eat small sharks of all kinds. And, like the hammerheads, they will also eat stingrays, completely ignoring the rays' pointed, poisonous

Objects Swallowed by Sharks

Spotted Eagle Ray

spines, which do not seem to have any effect on them at all. A tiger shark was once watched as it circled a stingray, apparently looking for an opening. When it darted in and seized the creature, it paid no attention to the furiously lashing tail with its wicked spine. One tiger shark was caught that had part of a spine, driven tight as a nail into its lower jaw, among its teeth.

A tiger shark was once a "witness" in a real-life murder mystery. In Australia in 1935, a fisherman put out a baited line about a mile from a place known as Coogee Beach. During the night, a small shark swallowed the bait and was, of course, caught on the hook. The next morning, the fisherman found that a 14-foot tiger shark had swallowed the smaller shark and was now caught on the line.

The fisherman dragged this huge catch ashore. Some time later, it was discovered that the shark had a man's arm in its stomach. The Australian police were called upon to try to identify the man, and from fingerprints they identified him as a man named James Smith, who was a known criminal. When the police began to investigate, they found that Smith had been missing for several days, and had last been seen with a man named Patrick Brady. Brady was picked up for questioning, and the police became convinced that he had murdered Smith and tried to hide the body in the sea. If it hadn't been for the strange capture of the tiger shark, the crime might never have been discovered.

The Whale Shark

IN THE warm waters several miles off the Pacific coast of Mexico, a rubber-suited diver, wearing an aqualung and carrying a spear gun, was swimming some 20 feet beneath the surface. The spear gun was equipped to fire small darts to which plastic tags were affixed, for the diver was a member of a scientific research team engaged in putting tags on fish so that their migration patterns could be studied.

Suddenly, the diver tensed. Moving slowly toward him, out of the green gloom, came an enormous, incredible shape—a dark, reddish-brown, streamlined body as long and as wide as a bus and covered with white lines and spots. A whale shark!

The giant creature slid through the water with ponderous slowness, only its tail moving gently from side to side. A swarm of black and silver pilot fish surrounded it, and as the big shark changed its direction slightly, to avoid the diver, the little pilot fish moved with it, almost as if they were robot-controlled.

The diver relaxed, for he knew that whale sharks were harmless to humans. But, curious and enthralled by the nearness of such an immense creature, he swam toward it. As he did so, the whole group of pilot fish took flight, moving quickly away in a flashing black and silver cloud.

The diver found it easy to match the shark's slow pace and began to swim alongside it. He stretched out a hand to touch the shark's sandpaper-rough skin, then, daringly, he took hold of the creature's back fin and allowed himself to be towed through the water. The shark did not act the least bit annoyed or frightened; it simply ignored the human, much as a human might ignore a pesky puppy that was tagging along. After a time, the man let go of the fin and, treading water, watched the huge shape vanish into the distance.

The whale shark is the biggest of all sharks. In fact, it is the biggest of all fish anywhere in the sea. A scientist who once had the opportunity of examining the body of a whale shark that had been washed ashore described it as "the most enormous, the most colossal, the most gigantic" sea animal that he had ever seen. These giants grow to a length of at least 50 feet, and some have been seen that were estimated to be as much as 70 feet in length. That's as long as many of the biggest dinosaurs were millions of years ago, and longer, today, than most kinds of whales.

Pilot Fish

Fortunately, these huge creatures are practically harmless. They feed only on tiny squid, small fish such as anchovies and sardines, and plankton. Plankton is small plant and animal life that floats in huge masses in the sea and is made up of one-celled plants and animals; baby crabs, shrimps, lobsters, and fish; tiny worms and jellyfish; the eggs of fish, squid, and other creatures. *Plankton* is a Greek word that means "wandering" or "floating."

When feeding, a whale shark swims near the surface of the water with its head pointed up, its tail down, and its enormous mouth—which is big enough for two men to crouch within—open. The shark takes in gulps of water which are then squirted back out through the gill slits on each side of its head. There is a kind of bony sieve, called a gill raker, in front of each gill, which screens the plankton, tiny fish, and other tiny creatures out of the water so that they are trapped inside the shark's throat and can be swallowed.

The whale shark is so harmless that it will let humans touch it, hold on to it, and even climb on it! A whale shark even let one scientist peek into its mouth. However, on a number of occasions, whale sharks have damaged boats by bumping into them and, at least once, a whale shark apparently *charged* a boat, hitting it with such force that it was turned around and all the crew were knocked down.

Unlike many kinds of sharks whose babies come out of their bodies, the babies of whale sharks hatch from eggs. A whale shark's egg case is shaped a bit like an egg-plant, about a foot long and 3 inches thick. The baby shark, about 14 inches long, is curled up inside.

The whale shark is the world's biggest fish, and the world's second biggest fish is also a shark—the basking shark. Basking sharks grow to as much as 40 feet in length. These creatures are a dark bluish-gray—often almost black—with whitish underparts. They have enormous gill slits that go almost all the way around their bodies, behind their heads. Because of their color and their huge gill slits, it's easy to tell basking sharks from whale sharks, even though they are much alike in size and in the way they act.

Basking sharks feed in much the same way whale sharks do, but they have slightly different "equipment" for feeding. Like the whale shark, the basking shark has gill rakers, but they operate in a different way. Like many long, stiff bristles, they lie flat against the sides of the throat when the shark's mouth is closed. When the mouth opens, they lift and fold back across the throat. This forms a mesh that strains tiny plankton plants and animals out of the water, but keeps anything bigger out of the shark's throat. Thus, the basking shark eats *only* plankton, and this means that it has to work rather hard to keep itself full, for it takes a lot of the tiny plankton creatures to make a meal for such a giant. A basking shark 22 feet long probably needs at least 2½ pounds of plankton an hour, so these big creatures spend most of their time just swimming slowly along with their mouths open, taking in food.

It is very likely that feeding basking sharks were responsible for many stories of sea serpents! Unlike whale sharks, which usually stay by themselves, basking sharks often swim in pairs, one ahead of the other. From a distance, they look like one, long, serpent-shaped creature. Rotting bodies of basking sharks, which have been washed ashore, have been mistaken for sea serpents, too, and one such basking shark carcass was once given the grand-sounding scientific name of *Halsydrus pontoppidiani* (hal-SY-drus pon-toh-pid-ee-AH-nee) because its discoverer thought he had found a brand new kind of creature. The reason for such a mistake was that most of the dead basking shark's cartilage skeleton had rotted away, leaving only its skull and backbone, and the long backbone, draped across the rocks on the seashore, resembled the body of a serpent. But when some shark experts looked over some of the backbone pieces of this strange "monster," they knew at once that it was nothing more than a basking shark.

Unlike whale sharks, basking sharks give birth to babies that come right out of their bodies instead of hatching from eggs. And unlike whale shark babies, which are only a little more than a foot long when they hatch, newborn basking sharks are good sized—at least 5 feet long. Basking shark babies are apparently born in litters, like cats and dogs, for a female basking shark was once seen giving birth to six babies that swam away as soon as they were born.

Now that you know that whale sharks and basking sharks are the biggest sharks, you're probably wondering which kind of shark is the smallest. It's a surprise to most people to learn that the smallest kind of shark is *very* small indeed—only a little more than 5 inches long! These tiny creatures, which have jet-black, cigar-shaped bodies, are called dwarf sharks. So far, they have been found only in waters near the Philippine islands and Japan.

Dwarf Shark

Basking Shark

The Bull Shark

IN THE country of South Africa, January is a summer month, and the weather is pleasant. On a January day in 1963, some students of the University of Cape Town set out on a canoe trip down the Limpopo River. It was to be a journey of about 120 miles, from a place called Guija, on the river, to Xai Xai on the seacoast. There, the Limpopo empties into the Indian Ocean.

The young men set out in high spirits, each paddling a canoe. The beginning miles of the trip were pleasant and uneventful; the canoeists joked with one another and enjoyed themselves.

But when the men reached a part of the river where the water was deeper, there was a change. They became aware of large shapes moving around them. Curved, triangular fins were cutting through the water. Sharks! Sharks were swimming in the river more than 100 miles from the sea!

Gradually, the big shapes moved in on the students. To these sharks, the canoes probably looked like some kind of big fish. They began to bump the sides of the canoes with their noses, as if testing to see what sort of creatures these might be, and whether they would put up a fight. The young men were suddenly aware of how

fragile their canoes were—nothing but a cloth covering over a wooden frame separated each man from the sharks!

Suddenly, one of the sharks attacked! It charged head-on into a canoe, biting savagely, and its sharp teeth sheared through the fabric. Water began to seep into the bottom of the canoe, and the man who was paddling it, faced with the possibility of having it sink and leave him swimming in water full of aggressive and apparently hungry sharks, began to paddle toward the nearest bank as quickly as he could. Fortunately, he made it.

To find sharks in a river, as these students did, is not really a strange or unusual happening. For although nearly all sharks are creatures of the salty sea, there is one kind of shark that is often found in the fresh waters of rivers, and even in a lake. Unfortunately, this shark is a very dangerous creature.

It is a heavy-bodied fish, gray on top and white underneath, and is usually about 8 feet long. It has a broad, rounded head, with very small eyes. The vicious teeth are serrated—that is, their edges are like the blades on saws. Because its broad head gives it a heavy, "bull-headed" look, this shark is

known in North America as the bull shark.

Bull sharks do not actually *live* in rivers, though apparently they often swim into them from the sea, moving upstream for many miles. A bull shark that was caught in the Atchafalaya River of Louisiana was 160 miles from the nearest salt water, the Gulf of Mexico, where it had entered the river. It is thought that bull sharks may become used to fresh water because they are born in the mouths of rivers, where the river flows into the sea and where fresh and salt water mingle.

In different parts of the world, the bull shark has a different name. The sharks that the South African students encountered are called Zambezi sharks, and they are feared throughout South Africa for having attacked many swimmers along the South African coast. They have been found in the Limpopo River, as well as in the Zambezi River from which they got their name.

In India, bull sharks are known as Ganges River sharks. The Ganges is a sacred river for Indians of the Hindu religion, and many of them make pilgrimages to bathe in its holy waters. Unfortunately, many such pilgrims have fallen victims to the sharks that come into the murky river. In one year alone, 20 people were killed, and probably a good many more were injured.

Sharks have also attacked people in the Tigris River in Iraq, in the Mideast. The sharks were not identified, but chances are good that they were bull sharks.

In Central America, in the country of Nicaragua, there is a large lake called Lake Nicaragua. It is about 110 miles long and 45 miles wide—and there are bull sharks in it. They are known as Lake Nicaragua sharks, and they have been in the lake for hundreds of years, during which time they have been known to attack, injure, and cause the deaths of many people.

For a long time, these sharks of Lake Nicaragua were a sort of mystery. Scientists weren't sure whether the sharks lived in the lake all the time, or whether they simply moved back and forth, from the ocean to the lake, by means of a river. However, most scientists are now quite sure that the sharks are just "visitors" to the lake, rather than full-time occupants.

Bull sharks belong to the requiem shark family, the same family to which the dangerous tiger shark and blue shark belong. But, as far as humans are concerned, in all that family of fearsome sharks, the bull shark may be the worst of the lot. However, despite the fact that bull sharks have been involved in many attacks on humans in many parts of the world, these sharks do not, of course, deliberately seek out humans as their special food any more than any other shark does. Their real food consists primarily of other fish, including rays and sharks, and they are deadly predators of all these creatures.

Some years ago, a 6-foot-long female Zambezi shark was caught and put into a large tank at the Durban Aquarium in Durban, South Africa, where a number of other sea creatures were kept. For 39 days, the shark refused to eat. Then, one day, a newly caught stingray was put into the tank. Almost at once, "Willie," as the Zambezi shark had been named (despite her sex), attacked the ray and swallowed it down. After that, Willie became the terror of the tank. She generally ignored the chunks of food that the aquarium attendants gave her, preferring, instead, to hunt the live creatures in the tank! During a three-month period, she attacked and ate a large, spotted eagle ray, a number of stingrays, some duckbilled rays, some skates, three dusky sharks, and five hound sharks. To make matters worse, she began to show signs of hungry interest in the humans who frequently came into the tank to clean it. Finally, she had to be put to death for being too savage a beast to associate with the more "civilized" creatures in the tank.

Thus, altogether, the bull shark seems to be a pretty nasty customer that isn't afraid of anything. Or is it? An interesting experiment that was made at the Oceanographic Research Institute in South Africa seemed to show that bull sharks might have an enemy they fear very much. It is known that sharks can hear and recognize a great many sounds and can tell the direction sounds come from. A tape of some sounds was played into a tank in which there were several different kinds of sharks. None of the sharks paid any attention to the sounds except for the one Zambezi shark in the tank. Suddenly, it seemed to become very nervous and began to swim around and around as if it were trying to escape!

The sounds on the tape had been made by a group of killer whales, a kind of porpoise that is a large and very fierce predator. Did the Zambezi shark get excited because it recognized the sounds of the killer whales and was afraid? Could it be that killer whales prey on bull sharks? If so, it certainly seems as if the bull sharks get what they deserve!

The Wobbegong

ITS EIGHT thin legs moving methodically, a small crab in search of food made its way over the sandy sea bottom in shallow water not far from shore. It was seeking one of the other many-legged creatures like itself (only smaller) that made the sea bottom its home.

A short distance ahead of the crab was a clump of brownish rock surrounded by a fringe of gently waving seaweed. The crab's beady eyes regarded the rock, and it began to move in that direction. It sensed that this might be a good place to find a smaller creature it could turn into a meal, for something might be hiding among the fronds of seaweed or in a crevice in the rocks. The crab scuttled forward until it was directly in front of the rock.

Suddenly, the rock seemed to split open, revealing an enormous mouth and rows of long, pointed teeth! With a lunge, the "rock" moved forward, and the mouth engulfed the crab. The "rock's" lunge carried it gliding through the water for a short distance, then it slowly settled back down onto the sand. Once again, it became motionless —a lumpy rock, lying among seaweed on the sandy bottom.

When most people think of sharks, they picture fast, active, sleek-bodied creatures that are always in motion, seeking prey. Many kinds of sharks fit that picture well. But the shark called a wobbegong is completely different in every way. It doesn't have a sharklike body, and it seldom moves at all. Instead, disguised as a rock, it lies in wait and lets its prey come to it!

The name "wobbegong" was given to this creature by the Aborigines, the native people of Australia. The wobbegong's body is thick, flat, and lumpy looking, and its head is broad, flat, and rounded. It has an enormous, wide mouth, and its eyes are tiny and partly hidden by folds of skin. Its body is usually brownish, yellow, or gray, and is covered by light and dark splotches of color which, along with its rough, bumpy skin, give it a rocky look. All around the wobbegong's head and mouth are little frills and tassels of skin that look like fronds of seaweed. Unlike most other sharks, which must constantly keep swimming in order to breathe and stay alive, the wobbegong is able to lie motionless for hours, with only its fringe of imitation seaweed gently waving like real seaweed. This not only adds to the creature's camouflage, it also helps to hide its mouth. And so, disguised as part of

Nurse Shark

the sea bottom, the wobbegong waits for its dinner.

The wobbegong's disguise is certainly good enough to fool the creatures it eats. Crabs, lobsters, and small fish will move right up to the "rock," only to find themselves suddenly being swallowed.

There are several different kinds of wobbegongs living in the seas around Australia, China, and Japan. Most of these creatures are rather small, but one kind often reaches a length of 10 feet. Wobbegongs are not considered to be dangerous to humans, but nevertheless, some of them have, at times, attacked people who disturbed them by wading in the shallow water where they lay. Unfortunately for people attacked by wobbegongs, these creatures are like bulldogs—once they close their teeth on something, they simply won't let go, and their mouths have to be pried open. In New South Wales, Australia, in 1953, a spear fisherman was *chased* by a wobbegong and suffered cuts on his face from the creature's teeth. It may be that the wobbegong was attracted by the bright metal band on the fisherman's underwater mask, but at any rate, as is the case with many other sharks that are considered "harmless," wobbegongs *do* sometimes attack.

Wobbegongs belong to the family of sharks that are called carpet sharks. You might think they were given that name because they spend most of their time lying on the sea bottom, like carpets, but actually it's because their skins *look* like carpets. The colored markings on a wobbegong's body often form really beautiful patterns of brown, violet, and lilac that sometimes resemble artistically designed Persian rugs or carpets. Because of this, wobbegongs are often hunted for their skins, which are made into leather.

But other members of the carpet shark family have no such claim to beauty. They are called nurse sharks, a name that has nothing to do with nurses or nursing, but simply comes from an old word, *nusse,* that means "big fish." Nurse sharks are a solid yellowish or grayish brown, and though they have the typical torpedo shape of most sharks, they are flatter and have wider heads than their relatives. Unlike any other kind of shark, nurse sharks have a sort of fleshy "whisker," like that of a catfish, on each side of the mouth. When these sharks are moving slowly, or lying motionless, these "whiskers" hang down, looking for all the world like two long, sharp teeth, and giving the sharks a sort of Dracula look.

Nurse sharks are bigger than most wobbegongs, averaging about 6 to 8 feet and sometimes reaching a length of 14 feet. Like wobbegongs, they often lie in shallow water on the sea bottom. But, while a wobbegong seems to prefer being by itself most of the time, nurse sharks often lie in clusters. With their heads resting on each others' sides and tails, they are like a bunch of kittens or puppies, or like pigs in a barnyard. They often lie so close to shore, in such shallow water, that their back fins stick up into the air.

Nurse sharks will eat small fish, crabs, shrimps, lobsters, sea urchins, and most any kind of shellfish. They have been described

Leopard Shark

in many books as mild and harmless creatures that are so sluggish they will let a boat bump into their heads before they will move out of the way. One scientist, a Dr. Gudger, told how his assistants used to catch nurse sharks and drag them up onto the beach where he would measure them and examine them for a time, then put them back into the water.

Despite all such reports about their harmlessness, however, nurse sharks, like wobbegongs, can be dangerous—especially if someone bothers them. Some years ago, a swimmer in Florida grabbed a nurse shark by the tail, just for "fun." The shark promptly turned and sank its teeth into his leg. Like wobbegongs, nurse sharks often hang on to something they have bitten, and the swimmer's companions had to pry the shark's jaws open in order to free their friend.

There is one other member of the carpet shark family. Living in Australian waters, it is called the leopard shark—not because it acts like a leopard, but because its back, sides, and fins are covered with spots that resemble those of a leopard. During the day, a leopard shark lies on the sea bottom, apparently asleep. At night, these sharks become active, moving slowly over the bottom in search of crabs, barnacles, and shellfish. Leopard sharks, which are often called zebra sharks, are not thought to be dangerous to people.

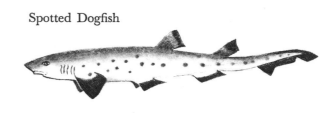

The Dogfish

Spotted Dogfish
Egg Cases

A SMALL female shark with a spotted body swims slowly through a broad patch of seaweed on the sea bottom. It is springtime—her egg-laying time—and it is among the plants of this underwater forest that her babies will come into the world many months from now.

As the female swims, moving in and out among the fronds of seaweed, the eggs begin to come out of her body, two at a time. They are strange-looking objects, for each egg is inside a hard, oblong covering that looks almost as if it were manufactured from shiny, brown plastic. Long ago, people who found egg cases like these, washed up on beaches, called them mermaid's purses because they closely resembled small coin purses.

At each corner of one of these cases there is a long, wiry strand, fantastically twisted into a number of complicated loops. As each case floats free from the mother shark's body, the loops catch on the seaweed so that the case becomes firmly anchored, as well as partly hidden, among the underwater plants.

The female shark finishes her egg laying and swims away. The egg cases hang suspended in the murky silence at the bottom of the sea. Within each egg, a tiny, big-eyed embryo shark waits to be hatched, nourished by liquid food stored up in the yolk sac attached to its body.

Time passes. The yolk sac shrinks away as food is taken from it into the growing baby shark. Near the end of six months' time, the little shark begins to twist and turn slowly. In time, it breaks through one end of the egg case and emerges into the world of the sea—a perfect miniature of its mother, only 3 inches long.

If it can escape being eaten by something, this little creature will grow to be a slim, 3½-foot-long shark with a brownish body covered with small, dark yellowish-gray spots—the kind of shark that is known as the lesser spotted dogfish. These sharks are also called rough-dogs or rough-hounds, because of their extremely rough skin, which has scales like tiny teeth.

Spotted dogfish are completely harmless as far as humans are concerned. They spend much of their time moving slowly over the sea bottom with their noses close to the sand, hunting for small crabs, squid, octopuses, shrimps, sea urchins, and worms. They do not hunt at all by sight, as some other sharks do, but depend entirely on

SPINY DOGFISH

Herring

Chain Dogfish

Spiny Dogfish

smell. When a dogfish's nostrils, which are on the underside of its head, tell it that it has come to something good to eat, the shark will stop, back up if necessary, and gulp the goody it has found.

The lesser spotted dogfish has a larger relative, the greater spotted dogfish, which grows to about 5 feet and has large, dark red spots. And there is also another relative that is known as the chain dogfish, because instead of having spots on its body, it has marks that resemble a chain wrapped around it. Oddly enough, these three *dogfish* belong to the family of sharks known as *cat* sharks! All the members of the cat shark family have some kind of an arrangement of spots, stripes, bars, or speckles on their bodies. Perhaps they got the name cat shark because these markings resemble the body markings of certain kinds of cats, such as leopards, cheetahs, and tigers.

There is another kind of dogfish shark that's called the spiny dogfish, or spurdog, but even though it has white spots on its body, it is not even closely related to the other three kinds of dogfish. It belongs to a completely different family. It would seem as if a shark has enough weapons, what with sharp teeth and sandpaper-rough skin, but the spiny dogfish has still another weapon at its command. At the front of each of the two fins on its back there is a sharp spur, or spine, which is slightly poisonous! The shark uses these spines to protect itself. By bending its body into a bow and then snapping its tail forward, it can lash out with the spines to puncture and poison whatever it is trying to defend itself against. It is from

these spines, of course, that the spiny dogfish gets its name.

The spiny dogfish is a small shark, only about 3½ feet long, and except for its spines, it is of no danger to humans. However, it is probably the most hated of all sharks—at least by the crews of fishing boats. This is because the little sharks often move in schools of as many as a thousand members, following schools of herring, cod, and haddock, which they eat. And when fishermen drop their nets, the spiny dogfish often cause all kinds of trouble. They may tear and bite the nets, and attack the fish that are caught in the nets, spoiling them as human food. Frequently, the fishermen find that the spiny sharks have driven most of the herring or other fish away so that when the net is hauled up, the only fish in it are hundreds of flopping, squirming spiny dogfish.

Despite this, the spiny dogfish is of considerable use to humans. In England, France, and several other European countries, it is used as food and is quite tasty. Much of the fish that is used to make the famous English dish fish-and-chips is actually spiny dogfish. Americans do not eat spiny dogfish (although they certainly could), but this little shark is widely used in medical research in the United States, and has helped scientists learn a lot about how certain parts of the body, such as the kidney, work.

Unlike the greater and lesser spotted dogfish and the chain dogfish, all of which lay eggs, spiny dogfish mothers all give birth to babies that come right out of their bodies.

And these sharks have the distinction of carrying their babies inside their bodies, before the babies are born, longer than any other kind of fish, amphibian, reptile, bird, or mammal. It takes nearly two years from the time a pair of these sharks mates to the time the babies are born.

Baby spiny dogfish are born with little stubby "caps" covering their spines, so that the spines won't hurt the mother while the baby is coming out of her body. The caps come off the spines shortly after the babies are born. Baby spiny dogfish are about 11 inches long. Aggressive little creatures, they have been seen to attack herring that were much larger than they were, only minutes after they were born!

The spiny dogfish has a relative that's sometimes called an alligator dogfish. These are good-sized sharks, often as much as 9 feet long, and scattered over their bodies are many curved spines, much like the thorns of a bramble or brier bush. Because

of these spines, the sharks are most often known as bramble or brier sharks, or simply spiny sharks.

In addition to spotted dogfish, chain dogfish, spiny dogfish, and alligator dogfish, there is an entire family of sharks known as smooth dogfish. They are small sharks, usually no more than about 5 feet long, that eat crabs, lobsters, and small fish. Like the spiny dogfish, they give birth to live young. And, like the spotted and spiny dogfish, they are supposed to be harmless to humans. However, at least one of them was once guilty of attacking a skin diver, who managed to beat it off and escape without serious injury.

So, altogether there are quite a few different kinds of sharks that are called dogfish. But *why* are they called dogfish? Well, long ago, sailors noticed that most of these sharks traveled in large groups—like packs of hunting dogs—and so the sailors named them *dog*fish.

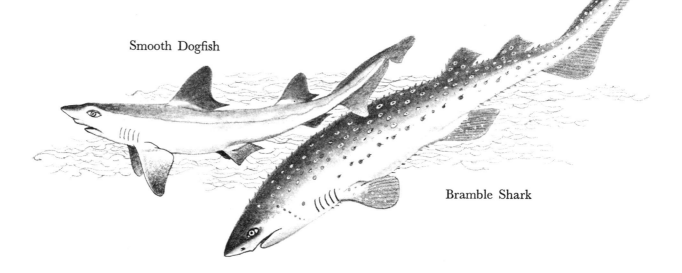

Smooth Dogfish

Bramble Shark

The Greenland Shark

FOR MANY miles, as far as an eye could see, the land stretched away, flat and white beneath a midnight blue sky that glittered with thousands of stars. But this vast whiteness was not truly land at all. It was ice—ice that was covered with a layer of snow. And beneath it was water—the water of the ocean that covers the North Pole.

At one place upon the ice there sat a small, white dome made of blocks of hard snow carefully fitted together. Half a dozen shaggy, wolflike dogs were huddled beside it, and a rickety looking sled made of bone and leather also stood nearby. The snow dome was an igloo, the winter home of an Eskimo family.

A man emerged from the igloo, crawling on his hands and knees out of a short, tunnellike entrance, and rising to his feet. He was a short, stocky man, dressed in clothing made of animal skins—a hooded jacket, pants, fur mittens, and boots of sealskin. The man glanced at the dogs, then stood in thought for a moment. He was badly in need of food for his family as well as for the dogs, and rather than go on a long hunt he decided to try for food that could be obtained without too much difficulty. Although it wasn't the best food that could be

had, he could get it right here on his "doorstep."

With an ax and a knife, the man began to chop a large, circular hole in the ice, revealing the gray-green water of the ocean beneath. Finishing this task, he dangled a bit of seal entrail in the water. He then sat back to wait. It was only a matter of time, he knew, until the scent of the entrails in the water would bring the creature he was seeking.

Time passed while the man waited patiently. And then there was a stirring in the water. A pointed, slate-gray nose poked up into the air. Without hurrying unduly, the Eskimo leaned forward and, reaching his hands into the water, seized the creature on each side of its head. Bracing his feet on the ice, he began to tug and haul, pulling a large, heavy body out of the water. Surprisingly, the creature offered no resistance whatsoever—made no attempt to either fight or flee. It acted much as if it were sound asleep and didn't even know what was happening to it! Slowly, with considerable effort, the man dragged it up onto the ice—a bulky, dark gray body longer than he was tall. It looked like a large fish, but in actuality it was a shark!

Although the ways of Eskimo life have changed, and most Eskimos have not fished for sharks in this way for many years, they once did catch sharks in just this manner. It seems strange to think of Eskimos catching sharks, for most sharks are creatures of the warm seas—creatures that are most at home among the colorful coral reefs and blue bays of South Pacific islands, or the sun-drenched waters of the Indian Ocean or Caribbean Sea. As a rule, most sharks only venture northward, to the New England coast of America, or the waters of Great Britain, when those waters have been well warmed by the summertime sun. But there is one kind of shark that makes its home all year round in the cold waters of the far north—waters which lie, in part, beneath the great sheet of ice that stretches to the North Pole. This shark is as much a creature of the Arctic as is a seal or a polar bear, and it seldom comes farther south than the places that are farthest *north* for other sharks.

Known as the Greenland shark, or polar shark, it is a fairly large creature, averaging from 8 to 14 feet in length, although one was once caught that was 21 feet long. It is a bulky, clumsy-looking shark with a rather small head, and with a small, curved back fin that is very different from the sharp, triangular back fins of most sharks.

Greenland sharks are also commonly called sleeper sharks because they are so slow moving and so sleepy acting that men in boats have actually caught them just by grabbing them by the tail. Because they are so easy to catch, the Eskimos, until recent times at least, depended upon them as an easy source of food, catching them in a number of ways. One way was to cut a hole in the ice, pour blood into the water, and then, when the shark came to investigate, the hunter would either harpoon it or seize it and drag it up onto the ice. It was also easily caught in the same way that small fish are caught, by means of a hook and line baited with a chunk of rotting meat or whale blubber.

And yet, even though the Eskimos found the Greenland shark an easy catch, they actually ate it only when they had to, apparently not caring much for its taste. As a matter of fact, its meat is *poisonous,* and if simply cooked and eaten it makes people and animals become quite sick. The Eskimos would boil it several times, or dry it over a long period of time, in order to counteract the poison. And for the most part, they used the meat only as food for their dogs. They also used the lower teeth of the creature as tools for cutting hair, and they sometimes made boots from its skin.

Greenland sharks seem to spend most of their time in fairly deep water, from about 700 feet to 2,000 feet. They eat cod, rays, and other bottom-dwelling creatures, and they will also eat any dead fish or animals they can find. In the stomach of one Greenland shark, the body of a reindeer was found. (The reindeer had probably fallen through a patch of thin ice and drowned.) Greenland sharks seem particularly fond of dead whales and will gorge themselves on whale meat until they can scarcely move.

However, a great many Greenland sharks

54

have been found with the fresh bodies of porpoises and seals in their stomachs, and it is obvious that Greenland sharks often swallow these creatures when they are still alive. This creates a small mystery. How can such a slow-moving creature as the sleeper shark catch such a fast-moving one as a seal or porpoise? Apparently, when it wants to, a Greenland shark can move very fast. However, no one has ever seen one do so.

There is another small mystery about these sharks, too. Most of them have a small kind of copepod—a shrimplike creature—firmly attached to each of their eyes. It would seem as if having something stuck to its eyes would make it very difficult for a Greenland shark to see and to catch food. However, old-time Norwegian sailors who fished for these sharks for many years and knew a lot about them, believed that the tiny copepods actually *helped* the sharks get food! The copepods have yellowish-white bodies that stand out against the dark gray or black of the sharks' skin, and the fishermen insisted that many kinds of fish and other creatures are eaten when they swim up close to the sharks to see what the bright white things are. Scientists are not at all sure this is true, however.

The scientific name for the Greenland shark is *Somniosus microcephalus* (sahm-nee-OH-sus myk-ruh-SEFF-uh-lus), which means "small-headed sleeper."

Skaamoog

An Array of Strange Sharks

A SHARK that glows in the dark! A shark that swells up like a balloon and barks like a dog! A shark that's "left over" from the world of 90 million years ago! These are a few of the other curious creatures that belong to the order of sharks.

In the family of cat sharks—the sharks that all have spots, stripes, or markings of some sort on their bodies—there are six kinds that are small, broad-bodied creatures about 4 feet long. They spend most of their time in shallow water and eat small fish, and they have become known by the name of swell sharks because of a rather peculiar habit they have. If a swell shark is caught and pulled out of the water, it immediately begins to gulp air until its stomach swells up like a balloon!

Perhaps the creature does this to make itself look bigger and more fierce. However, if the swollen shark is thrown back into the water, it must then float on the surface, like a bobbing beach ball, until it can get all the air out of its body again. This may take as long as four days.

Swell sharks are widespread throughout the southern parts of the Pacific Ocean, and it is said that the ones that are found near New Zealand bark like dogs! If so, the sound is probably caused by the air being pushed out of the sharks' bodies after they have blown themselves up.

Another kind of cat shark, one that lives near South Africa and is called a skaamoog, also does something rather strange when it is caught. It covers its eyes with its tail! For this reason it has become known as the shy eye. This shark's body is covered with markings that look much like a kind of ancient Egyptian writing.

Another shark family, the family of the spiny dogfish, contains a strange character, too—a shark that glows in the dark! Only a few specimens of these glowing sharks have ever been caught, as they live on the ocean floor at a depth of about 7,000 feet. They are small creatures, only a foot or so in length, and the bottom half of their body gives off a bright, greenish light. *Why* these sharks glow is a puzzle. They eat small squid and shrimplike creatures, and it may be that the light attracts these animals to them, making the creatures easy prey. Or, it may be that the light somehow helps the sharks to defend themselves, or serves as a warning to other creatures that the sharks taste bad. We really don't know. At any rate, because of their ability to glow in

Port Jackson Shark Egg

Goblin Shark

darkness, these little sharks have earned the name of lantern sharks.

The goblin shark is a strange-looking creature that is actually a "leftover" from the world of 90 million years ago when dinosaurs roamed the earth. It was discovered about a hundred years ago, when a Japanese fisherman caught a creature such as he had never seen before. It was fishlike, a little more than 3 feet long, and grayish-brown in color. Its mouth stuck out to form a sort of beak, somewhat like the beak of a bird, only it was filled with little teeth. And its snout stuck out even farther, being shaped for all the world like a trowel (the triangle-shaped tool that bricklayers use). The fisherman kept the strange creature and turned it over to scientists, who quickly realized that it was the same as a shark that had lived 90 million years ago and was known only from fossils. The scientific name for the goblin shark means "shovel snout." These sharks live in rather deep water, and not much is known about them.

The horn shark, or Port Jackson shark, which lives in shallow water near the southern and eastern coasts of Australia, is also a sort of "leftover" from prehistoric times— only it goes back even farther than the goblin shark, for it resembles a kind of shark that lived 150 million years ago. The back teeth of the Port Jackson shark are somewhat like a cobblestone pavement—rough, bumpy, and spiky—and the sharks grind clams, oysters, crabs, and other shellfish between them. Port Jackson sharks have a sharp spine, or "horn," sticking up at the front of each of their two back fins, and these spines give out a venom when they are stuck into something. The shark probably uses the spines as a defense against other sharks and large fish that might try to eat it.

The Port Jackson shark lays eggs, and they are surely the strangest-looking eggs in the whole animal kingdom. They are shiny brown, hard as fingernails, and shaped like corkscrews! It is hard to imagine why they should have such an odd shape. Some scientists think that when a mother Port Jackson shark lays her eggs, they may slowly *spin* and, because of their corkscrew shape, dig themselves into the sand at the sea bottom where they are protected until the baby sharks hatch from them.

As if two "prehistoric relic" sharks aren't enough, there's also a third kind of shark that resembles sharks of long ago. But this creature goes way back! It resembles the sharks of 350 million years ago—the very first kind of sharks there were! It is a snaky-looking creature with a thin, 6-foot-long body, fins that are like pieces of thin silk, and a head that resembles the head of a snake or lizard. Most sharks have five gills, like straight slits, on each side of the head. But this shark, like the first sharks, has six gills with edges that are wavy, like the frills on a fancy dress. It is from these gills that the shark gets its name—the frilled shark. It is also known as a lizard shark because it really resembles a reptile more than a fish. In fact, one of the first scientists to study it remarked that it looked a lot like a sea serpent is supposed to look.

The frilled shark is another deep-water dweller that probably feeds on octopuses and squid. Because of the way its head and teeth are formed, scientists think that it probably feeds much as a snake does—*striking* at its prey, catching the prey on its sharp, curved teeth, then sort of pulling itself forward to work the prey back into its long, snaky body.

And there are other strange sharks beside those you have just read about. One is the seven-gilled shark, and another is the flat-bodied angel shark, so named because its fins look like giant wings. As you can now see, the idea that most people have about sharks—that they're simply a kind of big fish that sometimes eats people—is certainly all wrong! There are more different kinds of sharks, with different shapes and different ways of life, than there are different kinds of monkeys, toads, and many other animals. And, like every other kind of animal, each kind of shark is simply doing what it must to survive in the great, endless struggle of life that goes on in field, forest, and sea.

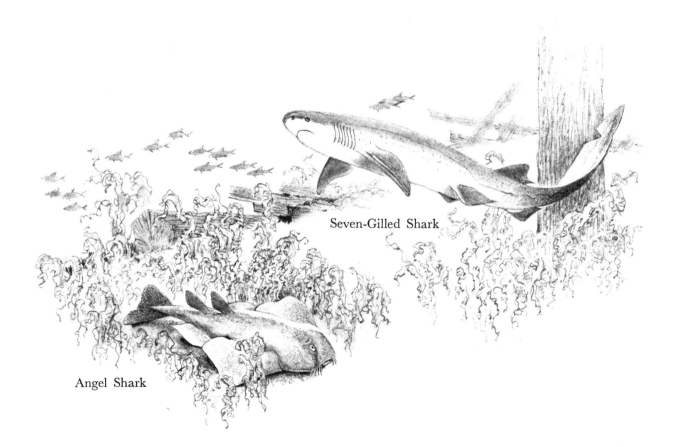

Seven-Gilled Shark

Angel Shark

Index